MY WORLD OF SCIENCE

Materials

Revised and Updated

Angela Royston

www.heinemann.co.uk/library

Visit our website to find out more information about Heinemann Library books.

To order:
☎ Phone 44 (0) 1865 888066
🖹 Send a fax to 44 (0) 1865 314091
💻 Visit the Heinemann Bookshop at www.heinemann.co.uk/library to browse our catalogue and order online.

First published in Great Britain by Heinemann Library, Halley Court, Jordan Hill, Oxford OX2 8EJ, part of Pearson Education. Heinemann is a registered trademark of Pearson Education Ltd.

Editorial: Diyan Leake
Design: Joanna Hinton-Malivoire
Picture research: Melissa Allison and Mica Brancic
Production: Alison Parsons

Originated by Chroma Graphics (Overseas) Pte Ltd
Printed and bound in China by South China Printing Co. Ltd

ISBN 978 0 431 13768 1 (hardback)
12 11 10 09 08
10 9 8 7 6 5 4 3 2 1

ISBN 978 0 431 13826 8 (paperback)
12 11 10 09 08
10 9 8 7 6 5 4 3 2 1

British Library Cataloguing in Publication Data

Royston, Angela
Materials. – New ed. – (My world of science)
1. Materials Science – Juvenile literature
I. Title
620.1'1

Acknowledgements

The publishers would like to thank the following for permission to reproduce photographs: © Corbis p. **28** (Paul Thompson); © Hutchinson Library p. **22**; © Paul Felix p. **16**; © Photodisc p. **27**; © Robert Harding pp. **8**, **18** (GM Wilkins), **21**; © Sally Greenhill p. **14**; © Science Photo Library pp. **10** (R. Maisonneuve), **26** (Wayne Lawler), **29** (Astrid and Hanns-Frieder Michler); © Spectrum Colour Library p. **24**; © Stone p. **23**; © Trevor Clifford pp. **4**, **6**, **7**, **11**, **17**, **19**, **25**; © Trip pp. **9** (N. Rogers), **12** (N. Rogers), **13** (P. Mitchell), **15** (N. Price), **20** (D. Saunders); unknown p. **5**.

Cover photograph reproduced with permission of Getty Images (Image Source).

The publishers would like to thank Jon Bliss for his assistance in the preparation of this book.

Every effort has been made to contact copyright holders of any material reproduced in this book. Any omissions will be rectified in subsequent printings if notice is given to the publishers.

Contents

Any words appearing in the text in bold, **like this**, are explained in the glossary.

What are materials?

The word "material" is often used to mean cloth. Scientists use the word differently. To scientists, "material" means anything that things are made of.

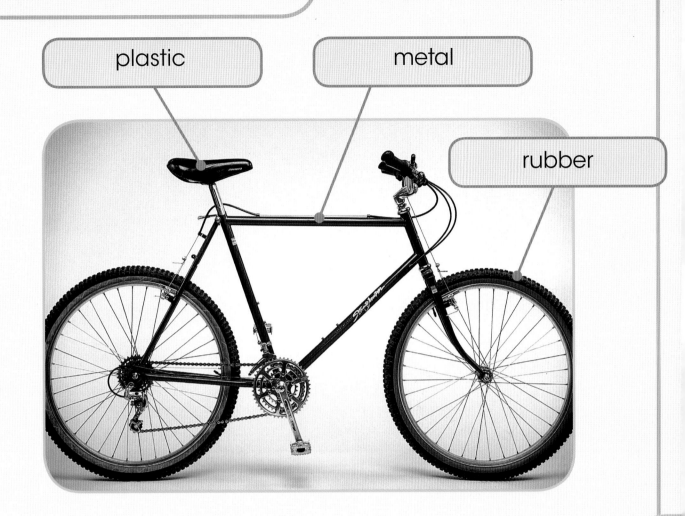

plastic

metal

rubber

This bicycle is made of more than one
material. Some things are made of one
main material. This book you are reading
is made mostly of paper.

Where do materials come from?

Materials are either **natural** or **synthetic**. Natural materials come from plants or animals, or they are found in the ground.

Everything in this picture is a natural material.

People make synthetic materials from oil.
Plastic and nylon are two kinds of synthetic
material. Some synthetic materials can
look like natural ones.

Wood

Wood is a **natural** material. It comes from trees. Some trees are grown to be cut down. They are used to make many different things.

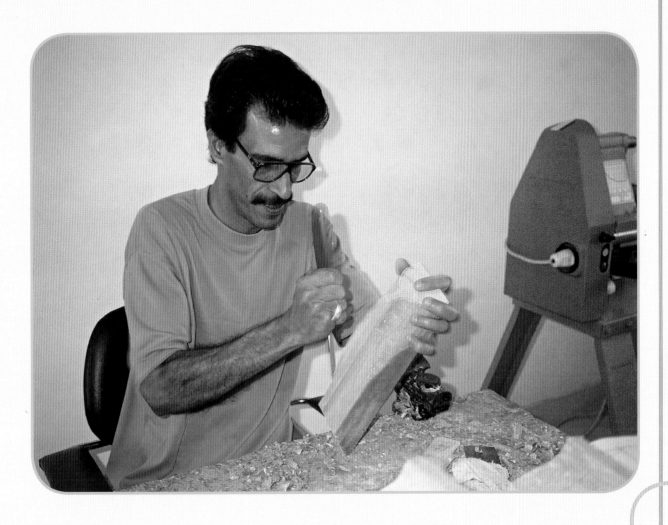

It is easy to cut wood into different shapes.
Wood is strong, and it is not as heavy as
stone and many metals.

Paper

To make paper, wood is shredded into very small pieces. It is then mashed with water to make a **pulp**. This is spread into a thin layer. When it dries, it becomes sheets of paper.

Paper is used for many things. You can write on paper and colour it with ink or paint. Paper is folded to make books, magazines, and bags.

Materials from animals

Sheep have thick, woolly coats. The wool is shaved off and **spun** into balls of wool. This woman is spinning. Her hat has been **knitted** from wool.

After cows die, their skin can be made into leather. This pony's saddle and bridle are made of leather.

bridle

saddle

Rock and stone

Rocks and stones are strong and hard. They are used to build houses and other things. This house is made of stone and so is the roof.

Some stones are **rare** and very pretty.
When they are **polished**, they sparkle.
Rubies are red. What colour are
sapphires? (Answer on page 31.)

pearl

sapphire

diamond

ruby

Clay

Clay is a kind of mud. When it is soft, you can make it into any shape. Then it is baked hard and dried in a hot oven called a kiln.

All of these things are made of materials that come from the ground.

Bricks are made from thick blocks of clay. China is made using thin pieces of clay. It breaks easily.

Glass

Glass is made mainly from sand. The sand is heated in a very hot fire until it melts. This man is blowing the **molten** glass into shape.

Most glass is clear and transparent. This means you can see through it. Some glass is coloured and you cannot see through it.

Metals

Metals are found in rocks in the ground.
This gold miner is breaking up rock
that has gold in it. Gold and silver are
precious metals.

This aeroplane is made of aluminium.

Most metals are hard, shiny, and strong. Steel and aluminium are two metals that are used to make machines.

Rusting and rotting

Unless it is **treated**, iron slowly rusts. It turns brown and crumbles. Wood slowly **rots** if it is left outside in the damp air.

Iron and wood are often covered with paint to stop them rusting and rotting. The paint on this ship keeps the water, rain, and damp air out.

Plastic

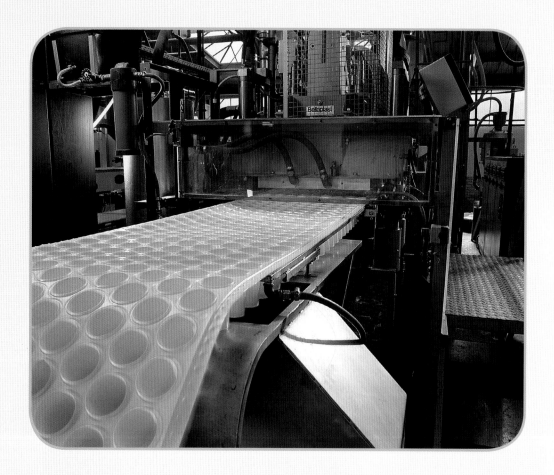

Plastic is made in a factory. Hot, runny plastic is poured into **moulds** to make any kind of shape. Plastic is cheap, light, and **waterproof**.

Some plastic is hard but some is soft and **flexible**. Which of the things in the picture can be bent or folded? (Answer on page 31.)

Clothes

Cotton comes from a plant. It is a **natural** material. Polyester, rayon, and nylon are made from oil. They are **synthetic** materials.

This cotton will be picked to be made into cloth.

Many clothes are made from cotton and polyester. The labels inside your clothes tell you what materials they are made of.

Recycling

Materials cost money to make. Some materials can be **recycled** and used again. Which materials go in these recycling bins? (Answers on page 31.)

Plastic bottles can be recycled and made into clothes such as this fleece.

Most plastic cannot be recycled. Throwing plastic things away causes problems because plastic does not **rot** or rust. Plastic rubbish lasts for a long, long time.

Glossary

flexible able to bend without breaking

knitted threads looped together to make
a cloth

molten melted

mould shape that can be filled with liquid. When the
liquid hardens, it makes the same shape as the mould.

natural comes from plants or animals, or found in the
ground

polished rubbed in order to make shiny

pulp material that has been squashed and mixed with
liquid

precious very valuable

rare not very common

recycle use again

rot become weak and crumbly

spun twisted into a long thread

synthetic not natural, made by people

treat protect something using special chemicals

waterproof keeps water out

Answers

Page 15 – Sapphires are blue.

Page 25 – The plastic bag can be folded. The straps of the sandals, the green file, and the drinking straw can probably be folded, too.

Page 28 – Plastic bottles, newspapers and magazines, glass bottles, and drink cans go in the recycling bins.

More books to read

Materials: What Is Stuff Made Of? (Ticktock Media, 2005)

Materials: Wood, Chris Oxlade (Heinemann Library, 2002)

Using Materials: How We Use Plastic, Chris Oxlade (Heinemann Library, 2004)

Index